Competency In ADHD Management

A Comprehensive Framework to Understanding ADHD

Joshy Degb

Contents

Introduction: Redefining ADHD

A Holistic Approach to Understanding ADHD

Significant advancements have been made in the understanding and management of attention deficit hyperactivity disorder (ADHD) in the rapidly evolving field of mental health. For a comprehensive understanding of ADHD management, it is crucial to embrace a holistic approach that considers the interconnections between **neurological factors, mental and emotional well-being, and practical strategies for daily living**. This comprehensive framework aims to provide a clear and objective understanding of ADHD. It is designed to address the complexities of the disorder and resonate with both the scientific community and individuals directly affected by it. ADHD is commonly perceived in a limited manner, with a primary emphasis on hyperactivity and inattentiveness.

However, this narrow viewpoint does not fully encompass the diverse range of experiences of individuals with ADHD. An all-encompassing perspective on ADHD acknowledges the deep connections between physical well-being, mental health, emotional equilibrium, and practical strategies for daily functioning. Recent research suggests that there is a strong correlation between gut health and brain function, specifically in relation to ADHD symptoms. A study published in the Journal of Psychiatric Research has revealed that children diagnosed with ADHD exhibit distinct differences in their gut microbiota compositions when compared to their non-ADHD counterparts. This finding suggests that there may be potential for dietary interventions to be explored in the management of ADHD.

Emotional and mental health play a vital role in the comprehensive management of ADHD. People diagnosed with ADHD have an increased likelihood of developing additional conditions, including anxiety and depression. The significance of integrated therapeutic approaches that target both ADHD and its emotional consequences is highlighted by this interrelation. One effective approach for individuals with ADHD is **cognitive-behavioral therapy (CBT),** which has demonstrated promising outcomes in addressing both the primary symptoms of ADHD and the accompanying emotional difficulties. Let's examine the case of John, a 30-year-old entrepreneur who has been diagnosed with ADHD. By utilizing a combination of Cognitive Behavioral Therapy (CBT) techniques and mindfulness practices, John was able to effectively redirect his hyperactivity towards fostering creativity and innovation. This transformative process allowed him to view his previous perceived hindrance as a distinctive strength.

Practical daily living methods hold equal importance within this comprehensive framework. Various methods are available to address the challenges faced by individuals with ADHD, such as **organizational strategies, time management techniques, and environmental modifications.** These approaches are specifically designed to cater to the unique needs of individuals with ADHD. For example, the use of visual schedules and breaking tasks into smaller, manageable steps can greatly improve productivity and decrease feelings of overwhelm. Using color-coded planners and setting reminders on her phone proved to be effective strategies for Sarah, a college student with ADHD. These methods enabled her to effectively manage her academic responsibilities, resulting in enhanced performance and decreased stress levels.

Enhancing our comprehension of ADHD is greatly enhanced by incorporating individual narratives and practical approaches to achievement. These stories offer valuable insights into the various approaches individuals take to managing their ADHD experiences. These individuals with ADHD serve as a testament to resilience and adaptability, providing hope and inspiration to others. As an illustration, it is worth mentioning that Michael Phelps, who holds the record for being the most decorated Olympian in history, has been candid about his ADHD diagnosis. The narrative of transforming hyperactivity into a strength in the pool showcases the capacity for remarkable accomplishments when provided with appropriate assistance and tactics.

Support groups and online communities are important for the comprehensive management of ADHD. These platforms facilitate a sense of community and shared understanding, creating an atmosphere where people can share coping strategies and provide mutual support. The increasing availability of digital tools and apps aimed at assisting in ADHD management, such as behavior tracking apps and virtual therapy sessions, highlights the advantages of incorporating technology into a comprehensive approach.

To achieve a successful life with ADHD, it is important to adopt a comprehensive and multifaceted framework. By recognizing the **connection between the mind and body**, attending to emotional and mental health concerns, utilizing practical strategies for daily life, and incorporating personal stories and interactive elements, we can establish a more supportive and efficient environment for individuals with

ADHD. This comprehensive approach not only improves our comprehension but also empowers individuals with ADHD to live fulfilling, productive lives.

CHAPTER 1

INTEGRATIVE METHODOLOGIES' POWER

Integrative methodologies for managing ADHD (Attention-Deficit/Hyperactivity Disorder) involve a comprehensive approach that combines conventional medical treatments with complementary therapies. This approach aims to address the complex nature of the disorder. This comprehensive framework acknowledges that ADHD is not solely a behavioral concern but rather a multifaceted condition that impacts multiple facets of an individual's life, encompassing cognitive function, emotional well-being, social interactions, and overall quality of life. Through the utilization of integrative methodologies, a treatment plan can be developed to effectively address the specific requirements of individuals with ADHD in a personalized manner.

ADHD management typically involves the use of stimulant medications like methylphenidate and amphetamines. These medications have been proven to effectively reduce core symptoms such as inattention, hyperactivity, and impulsivity. Nevertheless, it is important to acknowledge that these medications, despite their potential benefits, do have certain limitations and may result in some side effects. Integrative methodologies aim to improve the effectiveness of conventional treatments by incorporating complementary therapies. This approach helps to address a wider range of challenges experienced by individuals with ADHD.

The mind-body connection is a fundamental principle of integrative methodologies. ADHD is now widely recognized as a **disorder that affects the brain's neurotransmitter systems**, leading to physical symptoms and behaviors that impact the entire body. For example, dietary interventions can have a significant impact on the management of ADHD symptoms. Studies have indicated that specific dietary patterns, characterized by a high intake of refined sugars and artificial additives, may worsen symptoms associated with ADHD. On the other hand, diets that are abundant in omega-

3 fatty acids, lean proteins, and complex carbohydrates have been shown to have **a positive impact on mood stability and cognitive function improvement**. Incorporating nutritional counseling into the management of ADHD can offer a comprehensive approach to treatment.

Physical activity is an essential aspect of integrative ADHD management, alongside dietary interventions. Research has shown that engaging in regular exercise can have positive effects on attention, executive function, and behavioral regulation in individuals diagnosed with ADHD. Engaging in activities such as aerobic exercise, yoga, and martial arts can have a positive impact on both physical health and mental well-being. These activities not only *improve physical fitness but also contribute to mental clarity and emotional balance.* Physical activity has been found to enhance the levels of neurotransmitters such as dopamine and norepinephrine. These neurotransmitters are frequently lacking in individuals with ADHD, and by increasing their levels, exercise can effectively alleviate symptoms and enhance overall functioning.

Behavioral therapies are an essential component of the integrative approach. Extensive research has been conducted on cognitive-behavioral therapy (CBT), which has consistently demonstrated its effectiveness in assisting individuals with ADHD in developing coping strategies, enhancing time management skills, and mitigating negative thought patterns. Combining CBT with mindfulness-based interventions can be highly advantageous, as it helps individuals ***cultivate self-awareness and concentrate on the present moment.*** Mindfulness practices have demonstrated their effectiveness in reducing stress, enhancing emotional regulation, and improving attention span. As a result, they have become valuable tools in the comprehensive management of ADHD.

In addition, integrative methodologies highlight the significance of social support and the involvement of family members. Attention Deficit Hyperactivity Disorder (ADHD) has a significant impact on not just the person diagnosed with it but also on their family, friends, and wider social circle. Family therapy and parent training programs provide individuals with the necessary skills and knowledge to effectively support their loved ones. These programs provide parents with the knowledge and skills to establish structured environments, implement consistent routines, and employ positive reinforcement strategies to promote desired behaviors. Creating a nurturing and empathetic household can greatly improve the efficacy of strategies for managing ADHD.

Education interventions are an essential component of a comprehensive approach to managing ADHD. Children and adolescents diagnosed with Attention Deficit Hyperactivity Disorder (ADHD) frequently encounter difficulties in academic environments. These challenges can result in feelings of frustration, diminished self-worth, and subpar academic performance. Customized education plans, including **Individualized Education Plans (IEPs)** and 504 plans, are designed to address the unique requirements of students with ADHD. These plans offer accommodations such as additional time for exams, priority seating, and the utilization of assistive technology. By combining educational support with other therapeutic interventions, a comprehensive support system can be established to effectively address academic and behavioral challenges.

Furthermore, recent studies have shed light on the potential advantages of alternative therapies, including neurofeedback, acupuncture, and herbal supplements. Neurofeedback is a type of biofeedback that focuses on training individuals to regulate their brainwave activity. It has demonstrated potential for enhancing attention and reducing hyperactivity in certain individuals diagnosed with ADHD. Acupuncture, which is based on traditional Chinese medicine, has the potential to restore the body's energy balance and alleviate the symptoms of ADHD.

However, further research is required to establish its effectiveness conclusively. Studies have investigated the potential of herbal supplements like ginkgo biloba, St. John's wort, and valerian root in alleviating symptoms of ADHD. Nevertheless, it is of utmost importance to approach these alternative therapies with care and seek guidance from healthcare professionals to ensure their safety and suitability for each person.

Continual evaluation and modification of the treatment plan are essential for effective integrative ADHD management. Attention Deficit Hyperactivity Disorder (ADHD) is a condition that can vary over time, requiring ongoing monitoring and adjustment of interventions. It is important for healthcare providers to establish a collaborative relationship with individuals and their families in order to effectively monitor progress, identify any new challenges, and make necessary adjustments to treatment strategies. This approach is designed to ensure that the management plan remains relevant and effective throughout the individual's life. It is personalized and flexible, taking into account the unique needs and circumstances of each person.

In addition, integrative methodologies highlight the

significance of self-care and empowerment for individuals with ADHD. Promoting active engagement in one's treatment can cultivate a sense of empowerment and adaptability. Empowering individuals to navigate the complexities of ADHD with confidence and determination involves teaching self-advocacy skills, promoting healthy lifestyle choices, and providing resources for stress management. By considering individuals as active participants in their treatment rather than passive recipients, a more empowering and effective approach to managing ADHD can be created.

Integrative methodologies are highly effective in managing ADHD due to their comprehensive and tailored approach, which takes into account the complex nature of the condition. Through the integration of conventional medical treatments and complementary therapies, a comprehensive framework can be established to promote the overall well-being of individuals with ADHD. This approach acknowledges the significance of the mind-body connection, highlights the importance of diet and exercise, integrates behavioral and educational interventions, and explores alternative therapies. In addition, the importance of social support, family involvement, and continuous assessment is emphasized. In the end, integrative methodologies enable individuals with ADHD to assume control over their health, promoting resilience and lifelong wellness.

CHAPTER 2

THE RELATIONSHIP BETWEEN THE MIND AND BODY

How the ADHD Brain Is Affected by Nutrition

It is essential to comprehend the intricate relationship between the mind and body by understanding how nutrition affects the ADHD brain. Attention-Deficit/Hyperactivity Disorder (ADHD) is a neurodevelopmental disorder that manifests through symptoms including inattention, hyperactivity, and impulsivity. Research has shown that nutrition plays a significant role in influencing brain function and behavior, in addition to the well-established contributions of genetic and environmental factors to ADHD. The brain of an individual with ADHD functions in a distinct manner when compared to that of a neurotypical individual. This is primarily attributed to variances in neurotransmitter activity, specifically dopamine and norepinephrine.

Neurotransmitters play a crucial role in regulating attention, executive function, and impulse control. Imbalances or deficiencies in nutrition can worsen the difficulties experienced by individuals with ADHD by further disrupting important biochemical processes.

The role of essential fatty acids, specifically omega-3 fatty acids, has been extensively researched in relation to ADHD. Omega-3s are essential for maintaining optimal brain health. They can be found in a variety of sources, such as fish oil, flaxseeds, and walnuts. These components are essential for the structure of cell membranes and have a significant impact on cell signaling and neuroprotection. Studies have indicated a correlation between ADHD and reduced levels of omega-3 fatty acids. Supplementing with these essential fats has been shown to enhance cognitive function, attention, and behavioral symptoms in individuals diagnosed with ADHD. An example is a study published in the American Journal of Psychiatry, which reported that children diagnosed with ADHD experienced notable symptom improvements when they were given omega-3 supplements, in contrast to those who were not given the supplements.

Protein intake is another crucial aspect to consider from a nutritional standpoint. Proteins undergo a process of decomposition, resulting in the formation of amino acids. These amino acids serve as the fundamental components of neurotransmitters. As an illustration, it is worth noting that tyrosine and phenylalanine serve as precursors to dopamine, whereas tryptophan acts as a precursor to serotonin. Insufficient intake of these vital amino acids can hinder the production of neurotransmitters, which can worsen the symptoms of ADHD. It is crucial to maintain optimal neurotransmitter levels and support brain function by consuming adequate protein from sources such as lean meats, eggs, dairy, legumes, and nuts.

Carbohydrates have a crucial impact on brain function, specifically in the regulation of blood sugar levels. The brain depends on glucose, a basic sugar obtained from carbohydrates, as its main energy source. Nevertheless, there are variations in the quality of carbohydrates. Consuming simple carbohydrates, which are commonly found in sugary snacks and refined grains, can lead to sudden increases and subsequent drops in blood sugar levels. Fluctuations in mood, irritability, and difficulty concentrating can pose significant challenges for individuals with ADHD. On the other hand, whole grains, vegetables, and fruits contain complex carbohydrates that offer a consistent supply of glucose, supporting stable energy levels and cognitive function.

Micronutrients, such as vitamins and minerals, play a vital role in maintaining brain health and can have a notable effect on symptoms associated with ADHD. Iron is a crucial element in the synthesis of dopamine. Studies have indicated a high prevalence of iron deficiency among individuals diagnosed with ADHD, and it has been observed that supplementing with iron can lead to improvements in symptoms.

A study published in the Journal of Attention Disorders revealed that children diagnosed with ADHD who were administered iron supplements demonstrated noteworthy enhancements in attention and behavior in comparison to those who did not receive the supplements. In addition, zinc plays a crucial role in the regulation of neurotransmitters and the functioning of the brain. Research findings have shown that zinc supplementation has the potential to decrease hyperactivity and impulsivity in children diagnosed with ADHD.

Magnesium is a crucial mineral that plays a role in more than 300 biochemical reactions within the body. These reactions include those that are essential for neurotransmitter function and neural activity. Studies have shown a correlation between magnesium deficiency and heightened levels of hyperactivity, irritability, and aggression in individuals diagnosed with ADHD.

Studies have demonstrated that the addition of magnesium to one's diet can effectively alleviate these symptoms and enhance overall behavior. In regards to brain health, it is crucial to note the importance of B vitamins, specifically B6,

B12, and folate. Vitamins play a crucial role in the synthesis and function of neurotransmitters. Deficiencies in these essential nutrients have been linked to heightened symptoms of ADHD.

In addition, it is crucial to take into account the role of food additives and sensitivities when managing the nutritional aspect of ADHD. There is evidence suggesting a correlation between the consumption of artificial colors, flavors, and preservatives and the occurrence of hyperactivity and behavioral issues in certain children diagnosed with ADHD. The Feingold Diet has demonstrated positive outcomes in alleviating ADHD symptoms in certain individuals by eliminating these additives. In addition, it is worth noting that food sensitivities, such as gluten or dairy, have the potential to worsen symptoms associated with ADHD. Identifying and eliminating these triggers through an elimination diet or allergy testing can greatly enhance behavior and cognitive function.

It is also important to note that the gut-brain axis, which

refers to the two-way communication between the gut and the brain, plays a significant role in ADHD. The gut microbiome, which consists of trillions of bacteria, has a significant impact on brain function and behavior. This is achieved through the production of neurotransmitters, regulation of inflammation, and modulation of the immune system. There is a correlation between dysbiosis, an imbalance in the gut microbiome, and ADHD. Probiotics and prebiotics have been found to have a beneficial impact on brain function and behavior by supporting a healthy gut microbiome. According to a study published in the journal Neuropsychobiology, children diagnosed with ADHD experienced notable enhancements in attention and behavior after receiving probiotic supplements.

Proper hydration is an essential factor in nutrition that has a significant impact on the ADHD brain. Dehydration has the potential to negatively impact cognitive function, attention, and mood. It is crucial to maintain optimal brain function by ensuring adequate fluid intake, especially water. It is crucial to refrain from consuming sugary drinks and excessive caffeine, as they can lead to dehydration and worsen symptoms of ADHD.

Furthermore, it is imperative to emphasize the importance of developing healthy eating habits and routines for individuals with ADHD, in addition to addressing specific nutritional considerations. Consuming regular, well-rounded meals that encompass a wide range of essential nutrients is crucial for maintaining stable blood sugar levels, promoting healthy neurotransmitter function, and ensuring a steady supply of energy for optimal brain performance. Promoting mindful eating practices, such as consuming meals at a slower pace and minimizing distractions, can enhance digestion and optimize nutrient absorption.

It is crucial to acknowledge that nutrition is just one aspect of a comprehensive treatment plan for managing ADHD. By integrating nutritional interventions with behavioral therapies, medication, and other holistic practices, individuals with ADHD can achieve optimal outcomes. It is crucial to consult with healthcare professionals, including dietitians, nutritionists, and doctors, in order to create a customized and scientifically supported nutritional plan that caters to the specific requirements of individuals with ADHD. The correlation between nutrition and the ADHD brain underscores the significant influence that dietary choices can exert on cognitive function, behavior, and overall well-being. Various factors, such as essential fatty acids, proteins, carbohydrates, micronutrients, and hydration, are crucial for maintaining brain health and effectively managing symptoms associated with ADHD. By gaining a comprehensive understanding of the nutritional requirements of individuals with ADHD, we can optimize the efficacy of conventional treatments and foster sustained well-being and good health. Adopting a comprehensive approach that incorporates nutritional interventions alongside other therapeutic strategies can empower individuals with ADHD to reach their maximum potential and enhance their overall well-being.

Moving Towards Better Health with Exercise and ADHD

An in-depth analysis of the correlation between exercise and ADHD uncovers a significant avenue for improving overall well-being, emphasizing the intricate link between mental and physical health. Attention-Deficit/Hyperactivity Disorder, commonly known as ADHD, is a neurodevelopmental disorder that manifests through symptoms including inattention, hyperactivity, and impulsivity. In addition to medication and behavioral therapies, incorporating exercise into the treatment plan can greatly improve overall well-being and help manage symptoms effectively.

Exercise has a complex effect on the brain of individuals with ADHD, mainly by affecting the activity of neurotransmitters. Engaging in physical activity has been found to enhance the levels of dopamine and norepinephrine, which are crucial neurotransmitters that are frequently lacking in individuals diagnosed with ADHD. These chemicals are essential for regulating attention, facilitating executive function, and controlling impulses. Exercise can enhance cognitive function by increasing the availability of neurotransmitters, leading to improved focus, reduced hyperactivity, and enhanced cognitive function. This method of enhancing neurotransmitter activity provides an alternative to conventional pharmacological treatments, offering a comprehensive approach to managing symptoms of ADHD.

In addition to its biochemical effects, exercise also enhances neuroplasticity, which refers to the brain's capacity to reorganize itself through the formation of new neural connections. This can be especially advantageous for individuals with ADHD, as it can result in enhancements in learning, memory, and emotional regulation. Exercises like running, swimming, and cycling have been found to be highly effective in promoting neuroplasticity. Engaging in these activities has been shown to enhance the production of brain-derived neurotrophic factor (BDNF), a crucial protein that plays a vital role in promoting the growth and survival of neurons. Long-term improvements in brain function and resilience can be achieved through enhanced neuroplasticity, offering lasting benefits for individuals with ADHD.

The structure and routine that come with regular exercise can provide a stabilizing effect for individuals with ADHD. A significant number of individuals diagnosed with ADHD often face challenges in regards to organization and time management. Developing a regular exercise regimen can promote a feeling of organization and predictability, which can be especially comforting for individuals who value routine. Adhering to an exercise regimen can lead to improved management of daily tasks and responsibilities, resulting in a greater sense of control and accomplishment.

Physical activity is important for reducing stress, especially for individuals with ADHD who frequently experience increased stress and anxiety. Engaging in physical activity stimulates the production of endorphins, which are natural mood enhancers. As a result, it can contribute to a more positive mood and decreased feelings of anxiety. This can be especially advantageous for individuals with ADHD, as they may experience greater vulnerability to mood fluctuations and stress-related difficulties. By integrating consistent physical activity into their daily routine, individuals with ADHD can develop a healthier emotional state, which can improve their overall mental health and well-being.

Social interaction is a crucial component of exercise that can greatly benefit individuals with ADHD. Participating in group sports and activities offers valuable opportunities for individuals to engage socially, work collaboratively as a team, and enhance their social skills. These interactions have the potential to enhance self-esteem, alleviate feelings of isolation, and enhance social competence. Participating in team sports can provide children with ADHD with valuable life skills, including cooperation, communication, and perseverance. Group fitness classes or sports leagues can be beneficial for adults, as they offer a supportive community and foster a sense of belonging.

It is important to note the significant influence that exercise has on the quality of sleep. Sleep disturbances are a common challenge for individuals with ADHD, leading to worsened symptoms and detrimental effects on overall health. Research has demonstrated that engaging in regular physical activity can enhance sleep quality by effectively regulating the body's circadian rhythms and decreasing the occurrence of insomnia. Improved sleep can have a positive impact on attention, mood, and cognitive function, resulting in better management of ADHD. This creates a beneficial cycle that enhances overall well-being.

Incorporating physical activity into the daily schedule of individuals with ADHD necessitates a careful and personalized strategy. Choosing activities that are both enjoyable and sustainable is crucial, as it enhances the chances of long-term adherence. When it comes to children, it is important to include play-based activities like dancing, playing tag, or biking in order to make exercise enjoyable and captivating. Adults can achieve comprehensive benefits by incorporating a combination of cardiovascular, strength, and flexibility exercises into their fitness routine. Engaging in activities like yoga and Pilates can have a positive impact on both physical fitness and mental well-being. These practices promote mindfulness and body awareness, making them valuable tools for individuals looking to effectively manage symptoms associated with ADHD.

It is crucial to take into account the intensity and duration of exercise. Research shows that moderate-to-vigorous physical activity significantly reduces ADHD symptoms. Nevertheless, brief periods of physical activity can still yield positive results. As an illustration, integrating short exercise intervals throughout the day can assist individuals with ADHD in regulating their energy levels and sustaining concentration. "Exercise snacking" is an approach that involves incorporating brief and frequent periods of physical activity into one's daily routine, which increases accessibility and reduces feelings of overwhelm.

It is also crucial to establish a conducive atmosphere that promotes regular physical activity. Involving family members in physical activities for children can serve as a source of motivation and help cultivate a positive attitude towards exercise. Schools and communities can offer programs and facilities that promote physical activity to encourage participation. For adults, it can be beneficial to find a workout buddy or become part of a fitness group. This can offer accountability and social support, which can help maintain commitment to an exercise routine.

It is important to also monitor progress and acknowledge achievements, as this helps to sustain motivation and foster confidence. Utilizing a journal or a fitness app to monitor physical activity can be beneficial for individuals with ADHD. It allows for the establishment of goals, progress tracking, and motivation maintenance. Recognizing achievements, regardless of their size, can enhance self-confidence and underscore the beneficial effects of physical activity on one's overall health and happiness.

Incorporating exercise into the management plan for ADHD provides a comprehensive and efficient method for improving both mental and physical well-being. Exercise effectively addresses multiple aspects of ADHD by positively influencing neurotransmitter activity, promoting neuroplasticity, reducing stress, improving sleep quality, and providing opportunities for social interaction. Customizing exercise routines to suit individual preferences and needs, establishing a nurturing atmosphere, and acknowledging achievements can assist individuals with ADHD in utilizing physical activity to enhance their overall health and well-being. Studies have demonstrated the positive impact of regular exercise on ADHD symptoms and overall well-being. By embracing the mind-body connection, individuals can experience improved mental and physical health, leading to a more balanced and fulfilling lifestyle.

Managing the Symptoms of ADHD with Sleep

Understanding the relationship between the mind and body is essential to effectively managing the symptoms of ADHD through sleep. ADHD is a prevalent condition that impacts a significant number of individuals globally. It is characterized by symptoms such as inattention, hyperactivity, and impulsivity, which can pose various challenges. Sleep management is a crucial factor in reducing symptoms and enhancing overall well-being, alongside medication and behavioral therapies.

Sleep plays a crucial role in maintaining overall well-being, as it has a direct impact on cognitive function, emotional regulation, and physical health. Sleep disturbances are frequently observed in individuals with ADHD, which can worsen their symptoms. Studies have demonstrated that insufficient sleep can result in heightened levels of hyperactivity, impulsivity, and challenges with concentration, all of which are characteristic indicators of ADHD. It is crucial to establish and maintain healthy sleep patterns in order to effectively manage ADHD.

There is a complex relationship between sleep and ADHD. Insufficient sleep has been found to exacerbate symptoms of

ADHD, while the symptoms of ADHD can, in turn, disturb sleep, resulting in a cyclical issue. Individuals diagnosed with Attention Deficit Hyperactivity Disorder (ADHD) frequently encounter challenges when it comes to initiating sleep, maintaining sleep, and awakening in the morning. There are several factors that can contribute to sleep disturbances, such as delayed sleep phase syndrome, restless legs syndrome, and sleep apnea. These conditions are more commonly found in individuals with ADHD. Implementing specific strategies can greatly enhance sleep quality and alleviate symptoms associated with ADHD.

Establishing a consistent sleep routine is a key strategy for managing ADHD symptoms related to sleep. Maintaining consistency in your daily sleep schedule can effectively regulate your body's internal clock, facilitating easier sleep onset and wake-up times. For children, it is recommended to establish a consistent bedtime routine that incorporates soothing activities like reading or taking a warm bath. For adults, it is recommended to establish a consistent bedtime and wake-up time, even on weekends. Establishing a calming bedtime routine can effectively communicate to the body that it is time to relax and prepare for sleep, facilitating a smoother transition into a restful state.

Aside from regularity, the sleep environment also has a significant impact. An ideal sleeping environment for the bedroom includes factors such as maintaining a cool temperature, ensuring darkness, and minimizing noise. Improving sleep quality can be achieved by minimizing noise and light disturbances, as well as maintaining a comfortable temperature in the bedroom. Minimizing distractions is of utmost importance for individuals with ADHD. Creating an environment that promotes uninterrupted sleep can be achieved by utilizing blackout curtains, white noise machines, or earplugs.

It is crucial to implement a strategy of reducing screen time before going to bed. Research has shown that the blue light emitted by phones, tablets, and computers can disrupt the production of melatonin, which plays a crucial role in regulating sleep patterns. It is recommended to establish a screen-free period of at least an hour before bedtime in order to enhance melatonin levels, facilitating the process of falling asleep. Engaging in activities like reading a book, practicing meditation, or listening to calming music can promote better sleep hygiene instead of screen time.

The quality of sleep can be significantly influenced by diet and exercise. Consuming caffeine and sugar, especially during the afternoon and evening, can disturb sleep patterns. It can be advantageous for individuals with ADHD to monitor and restrict their consumption of these substances. In addition, engaging in regular physical activity can assist in regulating sleep patterns. Engaging in physical activity can enhance the body's requirement for rest and contribute to the regulation of the sleep-wake cycle. It is advisable to refrain from engaging in intense physical activity near bedtime, as it can be stimulating and hinder the ability to fall asleep.

It is essential to effectively manage stress and anxiety in

order to enhance sleep quality in individuals diagnosed with ADHD. Stress has a notable effect on the quality of sleep, resulting in challenges when it comes to both falling asleep and staying asleep. Practicing techniques like mindfulness, meditation, and deep-breathing exercises can be beneficial in reducing stress levels and promoting relaxation before going to bed. Individuals experiencing sleep difficulties related to ADHD may find cognitive-behavioral therapy (CBT) specifically tailored for insomnia, known as CBT-I, to be a valuable approach. The CBT-I approach focuses on identifying and addressing the thoughts and behaviors that disrupt sleep, offering effective strategies to manage insomnia and enhance the overall quality of sleep.

Parental involvement in sleep management is crucial for children with ADHD. Parents play a crucial role in ensuring their child's sleep quality. They can establish and maintain consistent bedtime routines, monitor sleep environments, and address any concerns that may be affecting their child's sleep. It is crucial to work together with healthcare providers in order to identify and address any potential sleep disorders. Conditions such as sleep apnea or restless legs syndrome necessitate medical intervention and can have a substantial impact on sleep quality if not addressed.

In certain situations, pharmacological methods may also be taken into account. Medication is not typically the initial approach for addressing sleep problems in individuals with ADHD. However, in cases where sleep disturbances are severe, it may become necessary to consider medication as a treatment option. One potential solution to assist in regulating sleep patterns is the use of melatonin supplements. Prior to initiating any medication or supplement, it is imperative to seek guidance from a healthcare professional to ascertain its suitability and safety for the individual.

To fully comprehend the connection between ADHD and sleep, it is important to acknowledge the reciprocal nature of this interaction. Enhancing sleep quality can have a positive impact on managing ADHD symptoms, while effectively managing ADHD can also contribute to improved sleep. In order to address this issue comprehensively, it is essential to employ a range of behavioral strategies, make appropriate environmental adjustments, and, if needed, consider medical interventions.

Utilizing educational and supportive resources can be instrumental in effectively managing sleep issues in individuals with ADHD. Support groups, whether online or in-person, offer valuable insights and shared experiences that assist individuals and families in navigating sleep challenges related to ADHD. By providing educational materials and workshops, individuals can gain the necessary knowledge and tools to establish healthy sleep routines and effectively address common sleep issues.

Effectively addressing the symptoms of ADHD involves incorporating sleep management strategies into a comprehensive treatment plan. Sleep is crucial for cognitive function, emotional regulation, and overall health. Improving sleep quality for individuals with ADHD can be achieved through several strategies. These include establishing consistent sleep routines, creating a sleep environment that promotes relaxation, limiting screen time, managing diet and exercise, and addressing stress and anxiety.

By implementing these measures, individuals with ADHD can experience significant improvements in their sleep quality. Enhancing sleep management can be achieved through factors such as parental involvement, access to educational resources, and, if needed, the implementation of pharmacological interventions. The relationship between sleep and ADHD highlights the significance of a comprehensive treatment approach that aims to enhance the overall health and well-being of individuals with ADHD.

CHAPTER 3

EMOTIONAL AND MENTAL HEALTH

ADHD: Using Mindfulness and Meditation

ADHD, also known as Attention-Deficit/Hyperactivity Disorder, is a neurodevelopmental condition that presents symptoms including inattention, hyperactivity, and impulsivity. The symptoms mentioned can have a significant impact on a person's daily life, including their academic performance, work efficiency, and social interactions. Traditional treatments such as medication and behavioral therapy are widely utilized, but there is an increasing focus on alternative approaches that aim to address emotional and mental health in a holistic manner. Mindfulness and meditation have been widely recognized for their potential benefits in managing symptoms of ADHD.

Mindfulness is a practice that originates from ancient meditation traditions. It entails directing one's attention to the present moment with intention, without any form of judgment. This practice promotes the cultivation of self-awareness and acceptance by encouraging individuals to observe their thoughts, feelings, and bodily sensations as they arise. This practice can provide significant benefits for individuals with ADHD. Individuals with ADHD commonly experience challenges in maintaining focus and presence due to a tendency toward a scattered mind. Mindfulness can effectively counteract these challenges by training the mind to maintain focus on the present moment. As a result, concentration is enhanced and impulsivity is reduced.

Meditation is a comprehensive practice that encompasses mindfulness and employs various techniques to foster relaxation, cultivate internal energy, and nurture qualities such as compassion, love, patience, generosity, and forgiveness. There are various forms of meditation, including guided meditation, mantra meditation, and mindfulness meditation. Each of these techniques has distinct advantages for individuals with ADHD. For example, guided meditation, which entails following the guidance of an instructor or an audio recording, can be beneficial for individuals with ADHD. It provides a sense of structure and direction, facilitating increased engagement and focus.

Scientific research provides strong evidence for the effectiveness of mindfulness and meditation in the management of ADHD. Research has demonstrated that implementing these practices can result in notable alterations in both the structure and function of the brain. For instance, studies have shown that mindfulness meditation can enhance the density of gray matter in brain regions linked to cognitive functions such as learning, memory, emotional regulation, and self-referential processing. These modifications have the potential to improve cognitive function, a common area of impairment in individuals with ADHD.

In addition, it has been found that practicing mindfulness and meditation can effectively alleviate stress and anxiety, which are frequently experienced by individuals with ADHD. Long-term stress and anxiety can worsen the symptoms of

ADHD, leading to a challenging cycle that is hard to overcome. Mindfulness and meditation can contribute to improved emotional and mental health by promoting a state of calm and relaxation. These practices promote a calm and composed approach to thoughts and feelings, which can help to lessen the emotional reactivity commonly associated with ADHD.

Incorporating mindfulness and meditation into daily routines can pose challenges for individuals with ADHD, given their inherent struggles with focus and consistency. With consistent and dedicated practice, the benefits will become increasingly evident. Commencing with brief, manageable sessions and progressively extending the duration can facilitate a smoother transition. Consistently dedicating a few minutes each day to mindfulness practice can result in substantial benefits in the long run.

Research has indicated that mindfulness-based interventions (MBIs) tailored for individuals with ADHD have demonstrated encouraging outcomes. Programs like

Mindfulness-Based Stress Reduction (MBSR) and Mindfulness-Based Cognitive Therapy (MBCT) have been modified to cater to the specific requirements of individuals with ADHD. These programs usually consist of weekly sessions and daily home practice. They aim to teach participants a range of mindfulness techniques and support them in incorporating these practices into their daily routines. Aside from structured programs, there are numerous resources accessible to individuals who wish to delve into mindfulness and meditation independently. Guidance and support can be found through various resources, such as books, online courses, mobile apps, and local meditation groups. Mobile applications have gained popularity due to their widespread availability and user-friendly interfaces. Applications such as Headspace, Calm, and Insight Timer provide guided meditations, mindfulness exercises, and progress tracking tools. These resources can assist individuals with ADHD in seamlessly integrating these practices into their daily routines.

Parents and caregivers of children with ADHD can also play a vital role in promoting mindfulness and meditation practices. Presenting these techniques in a formal and clear manner can assist children in cultivating a favorable connection with mindfulness. Activities such as mindful breathing, body scans, and guided imagery can be modified to align with a child's age and interests. Many educational institutions are now acknowledging the advantages of mindfulness and integrating mindfulness programs into their curricula. These programs aim to assist students in effectively managing stress, enhancing focus, and improving behavior.

Although mindfulness and meditation do not provide a cure for ADHD, they can be beneficial in managing its symptoms and enhancing emotional and mental well-being. These practices can enhance traditional treatments, offering a comprehensive approach to managing ADHD. Mindfulness and meditation can provide individuals with ADHD with the tools to navigate the challenges of their condition more effectively. By fostering self-awareness, emotional regulation, and cognitive flexibility, these practices promote greater ease and resilience.

When engaging in mindfulness and meditation practices, it is crucial to maintain a practical mindset and cultivate patience. It is important to note that the benefits of this treatment may not be immediately apparent. It may take some time for individuals to observe significant improvements in their symptoms. Consistency is crucial, and it is important to acknowledge and appreciate even the smallest steps towards progress. Engaging with a supportive community, whether through online forums, meditation groups, or therapy sessions, can offer motivation and encouragement.

It is recommended that healthcare providers consider integrating mindfulness and meditation techniques into their treatment plans for patients with ADHD. Through engaging in discussions with patients and offering them resources and referrals, healthcare providers can facilitate a more comprehensive and tailored approach to managing ADHD. Effective and sustainable outcomes can be achieved through collaboration among medical professionals, mindfulness instructors, and patients.

Mindfulness and meditation provide effective strategies for managing symptoms of ADHD and improving emotional and mental well-being. These practices are effective in promoting a state of present-moment awareness and acceptance, which can help individuals with ADHD improve their focus, reduce impulsivity, and better manage stress and anxiety. Although they are not considered standalone treatments, they can greatly enhance traditional approaches by offering a comprehensive framework for addressing the challenges associated with ADHD. Through regular practice and guidance, individuals with ADHD can develop mindfulness and meditation skills that can enhance their overall well-being and satisfaction in life.

How Cognitive-Behavioral Therapy Can Help You Manage Your Emotions

Cognitive-behavioral therapy (CBT) is a well-established and evidence-based method for effectively addressing emotional and mental health concerns. This therapeutic approach emphasizes the relationship between thoughts, feelings, and behaviors. It provides a structured and goal-oriented framework for comprehending and resolving emotional difficulties. Through an examination of the impact of cognitive processes on emotional responses and behaviors, CBT enables individuals to cultivate more constructive thought patterns, leading to improved emotional regulation and overall well-being.

Cognitive-behavioral therapy (CBT) is based on the fundamental understanding that our thoughts have a profound impact on our emotions and actions. Emotional distress and maladaptive behaviors can result from negative or distorted thinking patterns. As an example, individuals who consistently perceive themselves as having no value may encounter symptoms of depression and may choose to isolate themselves from social interactions. Cognitive-behavioral therapy (CBT) assists individuals in recognizing and transforming negative thought patterns into more positive and realistic ones. This process enhances emotional well-being and fosters constructive behavior.

Cognitive restructuring is a fundamental technique in cognitive behavioral therapy (CBT). It entails the identification and examination of negative thoughts, followed by the substitution of more balanced and positive thoughts. The process starts by acknowledging automatic thoughts, which are the immediate and often subconscious thoughts that emerge in response to situations. For instance, in the event of a test failure, one may immediately perceive oneself as a failure.

However, it is crucial to identify and analyze this negative thought. In cognitive-behavioral therapy (CBT), individuals are encouraged to critically examine their thoughts and explore alternative perspectives. For example, instead of thinking, "I didn't do well on this test," they might consider the possibility of studying harder and improving their performance in the future.

Behavioral activation is an essential element of cognitive behavioral therapy (CBT). This approach emphasizes the promotion of engagement in activities that provide positive reinforcement as a means to address negative emotions. Depression, for example, frequently results in a reduction of pleasurable activities, which can intensify feelings of sadness and hopelessness. Through the identification and scheduling of activities that provide enjoyment or a sense of achievement, individuals can effectively disrupt the pattern of inactivity and negative emotions. This approach has the potential to enhance mood and further support the notion that behavior can have an impact on emotional states.

CBT also highlights the significance of cultivating problem-solving abilities. People acquire the skill of breaking down complex problems into smaller, more manageable components and methodically tackling each one. This approach promotes a sense of control and effectiveness, which helps to alleviate feelings of helplessness and anxiety. As an illustration, an individual grappling with anxiety regarding a job interview could collaborate with a therapist to pinpoint particular concerns, such as apprehension about answering questions accurately, and devise strategies to tackle each concern, such as engaging in practice sessions for common interview questions.

Exposure therapy, a technique within cognitive behavioral therapy (CBT), has shown significant effectiveness in managing anxiety disorders such as phobias and post-traumatic stress disorder (PTSD). This method entails systematically and gradually exposing individuals to situations or stimuli that they fear in a controlled manner. Our objective is to gradually decrease the fear response by repeatedly exposing individuals to the source of their fear. As an example, individuals who experience a fear of flying can begin by observing images of airplanes, then proceed to visit an airport, and ultimately embark on a brief flight. Gradual exposure is an effective method for reducing anxiety by desensitizing individuals to the feared object or situation.

Cognitive behavioral therapy (CBT) is a versatile approach that can be customized to effectively target various emotional and mental health concerns. CBT is an effective approach for individuals experiencing depression. It focuses on challenging negative thought patterns and promoting engagement in meaningful activities, resulting in a reduction of symptoms. CBT offers individuals with anxiety disorders practical strategies to effectively manage worry and panic. Through cognitive restructuring and exposure techniques, individuals can develop the necessary tools to address their anxiety. CBT is a highly effective method for managing stress, anger, and relationship problems, making it a versatile approach for improving emotional and mental well-being.

Collaboration is a fundamental aspect of cognitive behavioral therapy (CBT). The therapist and client collaborate as a cohesive unit to establish objectives, devise tactics, and assess advancement. This partnership enables clients to actively participate in their treatment, promoting a sense of ownership and responsibility for their emotional well-being. CBT is a highly structured approach that focuses on setting goals and tracking progress. This structure allows clients to observe tangible improvements, which in turn strengthens their dedication to the therapeutic process.

Extensive research has consistently demonstrated the effectiveness of cognitive behavioral therapy (CBT) in a wide range of populations and conditions. Multiple studies have provided evidence of the effectiveness of cognitive behavioral therapy (CBT) in alleviating symptoms associated with depression, anxiety, post-traumatic stress disorder (PTSD), and various other emotional disorders. For instance, a comprehensive analysis of 269 studies revealed that cognitive behavioral therapy (CBT) demonstrates remarkable efficacy in the treatment of anxiety and depression. In fact, the effects of CBT are comparable to, if not superior to, those of medication. The extensive body of evidence has resulted in the widespread acknowledgment of cognitive behavioral therapy (CBT) as a highly regarded approach in psychological treatment.

Cognitive behavioral therapy (CBT) is available in different formats to ensure accessibility. These include individual therapy, group therapy, and online platforms. CBT is highly adaptable and can be effectively utilized in a wide range of settings and with various populations. Online cognitive behavioral therapy (CBT) has become increasingly popular due to its convenient nature and its ability to reach individuals who may face obstacles in accessing traditional in-person treatment. Research has demonstrated that online cognitive-behavioral therapy (CBT) can be just as effective as in-person therapy, providing a valuable alternative for individuals seeking assistance with their emotional and mental well-being.

To successfully integrate cognitive behavioral therapy (CBT) into your daily routine, it is crucial to consistently engage in practice and actively apply its principles. It is recommended that individuals maintain a thought diary to monitor negative thoughts and engage in regular cognitive restructuring. Participating in enjoyable activities and adhering to a schedule can contribute to the maintenance of progress in behavioral activation. Skills acquired through therapy can be utilized to effectively address various challenges in daily life, promoting resilience and adaptability.

Mindfulness-based Cognitive Behavioral Therapy (CBT), which combines mindfulness practices with traditional CBT techniques, has demonstrated potential for improving emotional regulation. Mindfulness entails directing one's focus to the current moment, free from any biases or evaluations. This practice facilitates heightened self-awareness of one's thoughts and emotions, enabling individuals to respond to them with greater efficacy. This approach can provide significant benefits for individuals who experience difficulties with repetitive thinking patterns and heightened emotional responses.

Cognitive-behavioral therapy provides a thorough and

research-backed method for effectively addressing emotions and enhancing mental well-being. CBT assists individuals in cultivating healthier cognitive patterns and coping strategies by examining the relationship between thoughts, feelings, and behaviors. The structured, collaborative, and adaptable nature of this tool makes it highly valuable for addressing a wide range of emotional and mental health challenges. CBT offers practical skills that individuals can utilize to improve their well-being and achieve greater fulfillment in their lives, whether it is delivered in person or online.

Building Resilience and Compassion

Developing resilience and cultivating compassion are essential for preserving emotional and mental well-being. Amidst a rapidly evolving landscape and the emergence of fresh obstacles, possessing these two attributes empowers individuals to effectively manage stress, bounce back from setbacks, and cultivate meaningful relationships with others.

Gaining an understanding of the principles behind developing resilience and compassion can have a profound impact on how we navigate the challenges that life presents, ultimately leading to an improvement in our overall well-being.

Resilience is commonly defined as the capacity to recover from challenging circumstances. Developing this trait is not limited to certain individuals but rather encompasses behaviors, thoughts, and actions that can be acquired and cultivated by anyone. Resilience is comprised of various elements, such as maintaining a positive perspective, effectively managing emotions, adapting cognitively, and having a robust support system. Developing these elements can assist individuals in effectively managing stress and preserving their mental well-being during challenging periods.

An important factor in resilience is the ability to maintain a positive perspective. Optimism does not entail disregarding the obstacles of life; rather, it entails acknowledging the capacity for development and favorable results in spite of hardships. Individuals who possess resilience often perceive challenges as valuable chances for personal development and knowledge acquisition. One effective way to cultivate a positive outlook is by engaging in gratitude journaling. This practice involves regularly recording things that individuals are grateful for. This approach redirects attention from negative aspects to positive ones, promoting a more optimistic perspective on life.

Emotional regulation is an essential aspect of building resilience. Managing emotional responses to stress in a healthy manner is essential. Practices like mindfulness and meditation have proven to be highly effective in improving emotional regulation. Mindfulness entails directing one's focus to the current moment without passing judgment, enabling individuals to enhance their emotional awareness and respond to their emotions in a more deliberate manner. Meditation has been shown to have numerous benefits, including stress reduction, improved focus, and increased emotional stability. These positive effects can greatly enhance one's resilience.

In order to cultivate resilience, it is crucial to possess cognitive flexibility, which involves the capacity to adjust one's thinking in accordance with evolving circumstances. The flexibility of this approach enables individuals to analyze problems from various angles and devise innovative solutions. Utilizing cognitive-behavioral strategies, such as reframing negative thoughts and challenging cognitive distortions, can effectively enhance this level of adaptability. For instance, in the event of a job loss, one could choose to perceive it not as a catastrophe but as a chance to explore a different professional trajectory that more closely resonates with their personal interests.

Building resilience is greatly influenced by having a strong support network. Interpersonal connections with family, friends, and colleagues offer valuable emotional support, practical assistance, and a feeling of inclusion. Establishing and sustaining these connections can assist individuals in feeling more secure and supported, thereby facilitating their ability to confront life's challenges. Participating in community activities, offering one's time as a volunteer, and fostering existing relationships can be valuable methods for enhancing one's support network.

Resilience is closely connected to compassion, both towards oneself and others. Self-compassion entails the practice of extending kindness and understanding towards oneself, mirroring the way one would treat a dear friend. It is important to acknowledge that errors are a natural occurrence and that no one is exempt from them. Imperfections are an inherent aspect of being human. Studies have demonstrated a strong correlation between self-compassion and reduced levels of anxiety and depression, along with increased emotional resilience. Practices like engaging in self-compassionate self-talk and participating in mindful self-compassion exercises can help cultivate this particular attribute.

Compassion for others, however, entails understanding and

a genuine intention to assist those who are experiencing hardship. By directing attention towards others, individuals can strengthen their social bonds and experience a positive impact on their emotional state. Engaging in acts of kindness and volunteer work offers numerous benefits, not only for those who receive the assistance but also for the individuals who offer their time and effort. It provides a profound sense of purpose and fulfillment. Developing empathy towards others can also help reduce the impact of stress and foster a more optimistic perspective on life.

Incorporating resilience and compassion into one's daily life necessitates steadfast commitment and deliberate action. Developing these qualities requires a gradual and consistent effort, as it entails making small and incremental changes over a period of time. For instance, dedicating a specific time each day to practice mindfulness, engaging in consistent physical exercise, and consciously making an effort to connect with others can gradually develop resilience and compassion.

Organizations and communities have a significant role to play in promoting resilience and compassion. Organizations that foster an environment of support, acknowledgement, and a healthy work-life equilibrium play a significant role in enhancing the resilience of their staff members. It is widely recognized that educational institutions that incorporate teachings on emotional regulation and mindfulness can play a crucial role in equipping students with essential life skills at an early stage of their development. Community programs that promote social connections and offer support resources can strengthen the resilience of their members.

It is crucial to integrate resilience and compassion into mental health care. Therapists and counselors have the expertise to assist clients in developing these qualities through proven interventions like cognitive-behavioral therapy (CBT) and mindfulness-based stress reduction (MBSR). These therapies provide individuals with the necessary skills to effectively cope with stress, overcome negative thought patterns, and develop a compassionate mindset towards themselves and others.

There are numerous advantages to cultivating resilience and compassion that go beyond personal well-being. These qualities have the potential to foster greater harmony and support in relationships, build stronger communities, and contribute to a more compassionate society. When individuals develop greater resilience and compassion, they are more capable of making positive contributions to the well-being of others. This has a ripple effect that can improve the emotional and mental health of those in their vicinity.

Developing resilience and compassion is crucial for preserving emotional and mental well-being. These qualities allow individuals to effectively navigate life's challenges with a positive mindset, emotional resilience, adaptability, and robust support systems. Enhancing resilience can be achieved through the practice of mindfulness, cognitive-behavioral strategies, and the cultivation of supportive relationships. Developing self-compassion and compassion for others can enhance these attributes, leading to a more satisfying and interconnected life.

By incorporating these practices into everyday routines, mental health care, and community programs, a supportive environment can be established that fosters resilience and compassion in both individuals and society as a whole. Embracing these qualities not only enables individuals to flourish in challenging circumstances but also cultivates a society that is more understanding and resilient.

CHAPTER 4

PRACTICAL DAILY LIVING METHODS

Time Management and Organizing Advice

Effective time management and organization are crucial skills for successfully navigating the intricacies of contemporary life. These skills have been found to improve productivity, decrease stress levels, and foster a sense of control over daily activities. Implementing time management and organizational strategies into daily routines can result in notable enhancements in both personal and professional aspects. Having a clear understanding of and effectively applying these techniques is essential for attaining a well-rounded and satisfying life.

Effective time management starts by understanding the significance of time and the need to prioritize tasks. Setting clear, achievable goals is a crucial aspect of effective time management. Having clear goals is essential for providing direction and effectively managing time. Breaking down larger goals into smaller, manageable tasks allows for incremental accomplishment, which is highly advantageous. This approach not only simplifies challenging tasks but also fosters a sense of achievement as each smaller task is finished.

An effective method for setting and achieving goals is the SMART criteria. The acronym SMART represents the following criteria: specific, measurable, achievable, relevant, and time-bound. By ensuring that goals meet these criteria, individuals can create objectives that are clear, realistic, and easier to track and achieve. As an illustration, instead of setting a broad objective like "get fit," a SMART goal would be "engage in 30 minutes of exercise, five days a week, for the upcoming three months." This approach offers a precise and quantifiable strategy, outlining a definitive plan of action and a designated timeline for accomplishing the goals.

Effective time management requires careful prioritization. The Eisenhower Matrix is a valuable tool for this purpose.

This matrix classifies tasks into four quadrants based on their level of urgency and importance. It provides a clear and objective way to categorize tasks into the following groups: urgent and important, important but not urgent, urgent but not important, and neither urgent nor important. By differentiating between these categories, individuals can prioritize tasks that are truly important and manage their time accordingly.

Tasks that are deemed urgent and important require immediate attention, whereas tasks that are important but not urgent should be scheduled for a later time. Tasks that require immediate attention but do not hold significant importance can be assigned to others, while tasks that do not require immediate attention and are not of significant importance can be removed or postponed.

Establishing a well-organized daily schedule is crucial for optimizing time management. Establishing routines is crucial for maintaining a consistent rhythm throughout the day and ensuring that no important activities are overlooked.

A well-organized routine can incorporate specific time slots for work, physical activity, meals, and leisure. Utilizing tools like calendars and planners can be helpful in effectively organizing these activities. Calendar apps and task management software provide added functionality, such as reminders and notifications, to assist in maintaining focus and efficiently managing time.

Efficiently managing both physical and digital spaces is crucial for enhancing productivity and minimizing stress levels. An untidy setting can result in disruptions and inefficiencies when trying to locate objects. Implementing organizational systems, such as filing cabinets for documents or digital folders for electronic files, can enhance workflows and facilitate the retrieval of necessary materials. Consistently decluttering and organizing spaces promotes the retention of only necessary items, leading to a reduction in disorder and an enhancement in productivity.

Time blocking is a highly effective technique for managing your time. One effective approach is to assign dedicated time slots for each task or activity. By allocating undisturbed time to a specific task, individuals can enhance their concentration and efficiency. As an example, individuals can allocate specific time in the morning for concentrated work assignments and reserve the afternoon for meetings or cooperative endeavors. This approach aids in avoiding multitasking, which has been shown to decrease efficiency and elevate stress levels.

In addition, it is crucial to acknowledge the significance of breaks and downtime in the context of effective time management. Working without taking breaks can result in burnout and a decline in productivity. The Pomodoro Technique is a widely recognized method that integrates scheduled breaks into the workday. One effective approach is to allocate 25 minutes for focused work, followed by a 5-minute interval for rest. Following four cycles, a longer break of 15–30 minutes is observed. These breaks offer a valuable opportunity for a mental reset, enhancing focus and boosting energy levels.

Efficient delegation is an essential element of effective time management. Assigning tasks to others, when appropriate, can help prioritize more important activities. It is crucial to assign tasks to individuals who possess the necessary skills and provide them with precise instructions to ensure the successful completion of the tasks. Delegation is a valuable practice that enables efficient time management while also promoting empowerment and collaboration among team members.

Procrastination is a frequently encountered obstacle when it comes to effective time management. In order to overcome procrastination, it is necessary to identify the underlying causes and then implement effective strategies to address them. Dividing tasks into smaller, more manageable parts can help alleviate the sense of being overwhelmed, thereby facilitating the initiation and completion of tasks. Establishing deadlines and implementing strategies like time blocking can effectively address procrastination by fostering a sense of urgency and providing a structured approach.

Efficient time management and organization necessitate ongoing evaluation and adaptation. It is important to regularly review and reflect on how time is spent in order to identify areas for improvement. One approach to addressing this issue is to track the amount of time being spent and analyze where it is being lost. By identifying areas of inefficiency, adjustments can be made to routines and priorities in order to optimize productivity. It is crucial to maintain flexibility in time management strategies, as circumstances may evolve over time.

Integrating effective time management and organizational skills into one's daily routine can significantly boost productivity and enhance overall well-being. These skills contribute to a more balanced and fulfilling life by reducing stress and creating a sense of control. Effective time management is built upon practical daily living methods, including goal setting, prioritization, and organization. By implementing various strategies such as the Eisenhower matrix, time blocking, and the Pomodoro technique, one can effectively maximize time utilization and enhance overall productivity. Consistent reflection and adjustment are crucial to maintaining the effectiveness and alignment of these strategies with evolving needs and goals.

Developing effective time management and organizational skills is an ongoing endeavor that has a profound impact on both personal and professional aspects of life. Creating an efficient and productive environment can be achieved by establishing clear goals, prioritizing tasks, and organizing spaces. In order to further enhance these skills, it is important to incorporate regular breaks, overcome procrastination, and delegate tasks effectively. Implementing these strategies can result in increased productivity, decreased stress levels, and a heightened sense of control, ultimately leading to a more balanced and fulfilling life.

Establishing ADHD-Friendly Environments

To effectively manage ADHD, it is crucial to comprehend the distinct requirements of individuals with ADHD and implement practical strategies in daily life that cater to these needs. ADHD, also known as Attention Deficit Hyperactivity Disorder, is characterized by symptoms including inattention, hyperactivity, and impulsivity. The symptoms mentioned can have a significant impact on different areas of daily life, such as work, education, and personal relationships. Creating environments that are conducive to individuals with ADHD can help address these difficulties and enhance concentration, efficiency, and overall welfare.

Minimizing distractions is a crucial factor in establishing an environment that is conducive to individuals with ADHD. People diagnosed with ADHD frequently experience difficulties sustaining attention and can easily become distracted by external stimuli. It is essential to prioritize the design of spaces that minimize potential distractions. This could potentially entail organizing physical spaces to establish a more structured and tranquil atmosphere. It is recommended to keep only essential items on desks or workstations in order to maintain focus on the task at hand.

In addition, the utilization of tools like noise-canceling headphones or white noise machines can effectively mitigate the impact of background noise, a prevalent cause of distraction.

Lighting and color schemes are important factors in the creation of environments that are conducive to individuals with ADHD. It is crucial to have appropriate lighting, as harsh or flickering lights can cause distractions and discomfort. It is recommended to prioritize natural light whenever feasible. However, in cases where natural light is not available, utilizing soft, ambient lighting can help establish a serene and concentrated environment. When considering color schemes, it is generally recommended to opt for muted and calming colors like blues and greens, as opposed to bright and vibrant colors that may be overly stimulating. These small adjustments can have a significant impact on how individuals with ADHD perceive and engage with their environment.

Effective management of ADHD requires careful

consideration of organizational strategies. Individuals with ADHD often face difficulties in maintaining organization, resulting in heightened frustration and reduced productivity. Implementing well-defined and efficient organizational systems can help alleviate these challenges. One way to improve organization is by implementing labeled storage containers, color-coded files, and designated areas for specific items. This system can greatly enhance the ease of locating and managing belongings. Digital tools and apps that are specifically designed for organization and time management, such as to-do lists, reminders, and calendar apps, can offer significant benefits. These tools assist in organizing daily activities and ensuring that crucial tasks are not overlooked.

Individuals with ADHD often encounter considerable difficulties in the realm of time management. Creating and adhering to routines and schedules can offer a valuable sense of organization and predictability. By breaking down tasks into smaller, manageable steps and utilizing timers to allocate specific periods for each task, individuals can effectively maintain focus and avoid feelings of being overwhelmed. One effective technique is the Pomodoro Technique, where individuals work for 25 minutes and then take a 5-minute break. This approach not only aids in maintaining focus but also offers scheduled breaks, which can help prevent exhaustion.

Accommodations can be implemented in educational and workplace environments to provide support for individuals with ADHD. For example, implementing accommodations such as extending deadlines for assignments and tests, supplementing verbal instructions with written ones, and allowing the use of fidget tools or standing desks can effectively assist in managing symptoms. It can be advantageous to have flexible seating arrangements and the opportunity to take short, frequent breaks. It is important for employers and educators to be aware of these needs and ready to implement reasonable accommodations to support individuals with ADHD.

Establishing an environment that is conducive to individuals with ADHD includes promoting effective behavioral strategies and providing emotional support. Promoting the utilization of positive reinforcement and establishing attainable objectives can enhance motivation and self-confidence. It is crucial to prioritize the development of coping strategies for effectively managing stress and frustration. Practicing mindfulness techniques, such as meditation and deep breathing exercises, can be beneficial for individuals with ADHD. These techniques can assist in managing emotions and enhancing the ability to concentrate. Therapy and counseling can offer valuable support by providing strategies and tools to effectively cope with the challenges associated with ADHD.

Managing ADHD symptoms requires attention to both diet and physical activity. A well-rounded diet that incorporates necessary nutrients can have a beneficial effect on brain function and overall well-being. Research indicates that specific foods and additives may potentially worsen symptoms associated with ADHD. Therefore, it is advisable to carefully observe and modify dietary habits as necessary. Engaging in regular physical activity can be beneficial in managing symptoms as it improves concentration, reduces stress, and enhances mood. Promoting engagement in sports, yoga, or regular walks can have a notable impact.

Having a strong network of support from family, friends, and colleagues is crucial to establishing a nurturing environment for individuals with ADHD. Providing information about ADHD and its impact can help cultivate understanding and tolerance among individuals. Individuals with ADHD benefit greatly from feeling understood and supported, as it enhances their ability to effectively manage their symptoms. It is important to acknowledge that creating ADHD-friendly environments is a continuous endeavor. Regular assessment and adjustments are necessary to ensure that the needs of individuals with ADHD are effectively met. It is crucial to maintain a flexible and open mindset when it comes to trying new strategies, as what may be effective for one individual may not yield the same results for another.

Developing environments that are conducive to individuals with ADHD requires a comprehensive approach. This entails reducing distractions, implementing effective organizational techniques, managing time efficiently, offering appropriate accommodations in educational and workplace settings, promoting positive behavioral strategies, maintaining a healthy diet and regular exercise routine, and providing necessary social support.

By gaining a comprehensive understanding of the specific requirements of individuals with ADHD, it becomes feasible to establish environments that foster enhanced concentration, efficiency, and overall welfare. These practical strategies for daily living are crucial for individuals with ADHD to effectively navigate the challenges they encounter and reach their maximum potential.

Stress Reduction and Burnout Prevention

Effective stress reduction and burnout prevention are essential for maintaining overall well-being, particularly in the context of practical daily living methods. To fully comprehend and effectively tackle these concerns, it is essential to adopt a comprehensive approach that takes into account different facets of one's daily existence, such as professional endeavors, interpersonal connections, and self-care routines. By incorporating efficient techniques into their daily schedules, individuals can enhance their ability to handle stress and avoid burnout, resulting in a more well-rounded and satisfying life.

Stress is a common reaction to difficult circumstances, but prolonged stress can negatively impact both physical and mental well-being. Common symptoms of chronic stress include feelings of exhaustion, heightened irritability, challenges with concentration, and a compromised immune system. When chronic stress is not properly addressed, it can result in burnout, which is characterized by emotional, physical, and mental exhaustion due to prolonged and excessive stress. Burnout is commonly linked to stress in the workplace, although it can also stem from various other pressures in life.

An effective approach to reducing stress is by implementing proper time management techniques. By prioritizing tasks, setting realistic goals, and breaking down large projects into manageable steps, individuals can effectively reduce feelings of being overwhelmed. Establishing a daily schedule that incorporates dedicated time for work, rest, and leisure activities promotes a well-rounded approach to daily life. Various tools, including planners, calendars, and digital apps, can be utilized to effectively organize tasks and manage time. Engaging in regular physical activity is a highly effective approach to alleviating stress and mitigating the risk of burnout. Engaging in physical activity has been found to release endorphins, which are known to have mood-lifting properties. Additionally, regular exercise has been shown to have positive effects on sleep quality, anxiety reduction, and overall energy levels. Integrating regular physical activity into daily routines, whether through structured exercise programs or simple activities like walking or yoga, can greatly improve stress resilience. In addition, engaging in physical activity can be a beneficial way to release tension and promote mental clarity.

In order to effectively manage stress, it is crucial to incorporate mindfulness and relaxation techniques into one's routine. Engaging in practices such as meditation, deep breathing exercises, and progressive muscle relaxation can effectively calm the mind and body, leading to a reduction in the physical symptoms commonly associated with stress. Mindfulness entails directing one's attention to the present moment and embracing it without evaluation. This practice can assist individuals in gaining insight into their stressors and diminishing their influence. Consistently implementing these techniques can help individuals develop resilience to stress and reduce the risk of burnout.

It is essential to prioritize maintaining a healthy work-life balance in order to prevent burnout. Excessive work can result in fatigue and reduced efficiency, while disregarding personal time can put strain on relationships and compromise overall well-being. Establishing clear boundaries between work and personal life is crucial for maintaining a healthy balance. It is important to refrain from checking work emails outside of office hours and to dedicate specific time for engaging in hobbies and social activities. By doing so, individuals can effectively manage their time and prioritize their well-being. It is crucial to incorporate regular breaks into your work schedule to ensure proper rest and rejuvenation.

Another crucial aspect of effectively managing stress and mitigating burnout is the presence of social support. Establishing connections with family, friends, and colleagues can offer valuable emotional support, practical assistance, and a feeling of belonging. Sharing experiences and feelings with others can be beneficial for reducing stress and gaining fresh insights into managing challenges. When individuals seek support from their supervisors or human resources in professional settings, they can often receive accommodations or adjustments that effectively reduce work-related stress.

The role of nutrition in managing stress and preventing burnout is crucial. Consuming a well-rounded diet that incorporates a wide range of essential nutrients can contribute to the stabilization of both mood and energy levels. Consuming foods that are abundant in vitamins, minerals, and antioxidants can contribute to overall well-being and bolster the body's capacity to manage stress. It is advisable to limit the intake of caffeine, alcohol, and processed foods, as they can worsen stress and fatigue.

Getting enough sleep is crucial for effectively managing stress. Chronic sleep deprivation has been found to have negative effects on cognitive function, leading to impaired mental abilities. Additionally, it can result in increased irritability and a reduced capacity to effectively manage stress. By implementing a consistent sleep schedule, optimizing the sleep environment, and adhering to proper sleep hygiene practices, one can enhance both the quality and duration of their sleep. Implementing certain strategies, like refraining from using screens before going to bed, maintaining a dark and cool bedroom environment, and practicing relaxation techniques, can contribute to improving sleep quality.

Participating in activities that bring joy and fulfillment is crucial for reducing stress and preventing burnout. Engaging in personal interests, immersing oneself in natural surroundings, and actively participating in artistic endeavors can offer a feeling of fulfillment and tranquility. Engaging in these activities can effectively alleviate work-related stress and contribute to the overall well-being of individuals.

Employers have the ability to greatly impact stress reduction and burnout prevention in the workplace by fostering a healthy work environment. One approach to addressing stress in the workplace is by providing resources for stress management. This can involve implementing employee assistance programs, allowing for flexible work schedules, promoting regular breaks, and cultivating a work culture that is supportive and collaborative. Employees can benefit from training programs focused on stress management and resilience.

Recognizing the signs of burnout and taking proactive steps to address them is crucial. Signs of burnout encompass persistent exhaustion, a pessimistic attitude, reduced productivity, and a sense of emotional disconnection. If the aforementioned symptoms are observed, it might be advisable to reassess the workload, consider seeking professional assistance, and enhance the implementation of stress management strategies with greater rigor.

Incorporating these strategies for reducing stress and preventing burnout into one's daily routine can result in notable enhancements in overall health and well-being. Through the implementation of effective time management, regular engagement in physical activity, mindfulness practice, maintaining a healthy work-life balance, seeking social support, following a nutritious diet, ensuring sufficient sleep, and participating in enjoyable activities, individuals can develop resilience against stress and proactively prevent burnout.

Efficiently managing stress and preventing burnout are crucial aspects of implementing practical strategies for daily living. Through the implementation of a comprehensive strategy that encompasses all facets of life, individuals can successfully navigate stress and achieve a state of equilibrium and satisfaction. Implementing these strategies can have a positive impact on emotional and mental well-being, as well as physical health and the overall quality of life. Continual assessment and adjustment of these practices are crucial to meeting evolving needs and circumstances, guaranteeing long-term well-being and resilience.

CHAPTER 5

INDIVIDUAL NARRATIVES AND PRACTICAL APPROACHES TO ACHIEVEMENT

True Stories of Overcoming Obstacles

Overcoming obstacles is a common part of the human experience that everyone encounters. Every person's path is defined by distinct obstacles, and the methods by which individuals overcome these challenges often become compelling stories that motivate and enlighten others. The stories presented here showcase practical approaches to achieving success, with a focus on the interplay between personal determination and the strategies used to overcome challenges. Within this context, gaining a comprehensive understanding of the intricate, practical experiences of individuals can provide valuable insights into the overarching themes of resilience, flexibility, and achievement.

An example that showcases the ability to overcome obstacles is the story of J.K. Rowling, the renowned author of the Harry Potter series that has gained worldwide acclaim. Prior to attaining recognition and accomplishment, Rowling encountered several obstacles, such as the unfortunate loss of her mother, an unsuccessful marriage, and financial difficulties while raising her child alone. In spite of the challenges she faced, she remained dedicated to her writing, frequently devoting her time to her manuscript in cafes as her daughter peacefully slumbered by her side. Rowling's journey highlights the significance of perseverance and confidence in oneself.

The narrative exemplifies the importance of unwavering dedication to one's objectives despite encountering numerous setbacks and personal obstacles, which can ultimately result in extraordinary accomplishments. Rowling's eventual success is a testament to the strength of perseverance and the profound influence of artistic self-expression.

Within the realm of sports, the tale of Michael Jordan stands as a compelling account of triumphing over challenges. Jordan is widely recognized as one of the most exceptional basketball players in history. However, his journey to success was not without challenges. During his high school years, he faced the disappointment of not making the varsity basketball team, a situation that might have disheartened most individuals. On the contrary, Jordan utilized this experience as a driving force to enhance his abilities through increased dedication and effort. Through his unwavering commitment to training and a relentless drive to succeed, he ultimately achieved an illustrious career in the NBA. Jordan's story emphasizes the significance of persistence and the ability to view obstacles as opportunities for personal growth and achievement. The individual's journey serves as a testament to the power of a diligent work ethic and an unwavering commitment to excellence. Despite facing initial setbacks, they were able to overcome these obstacles and ultimately achieve remarkable success.

Also, within the realm of technology and entrepreneurship, the tale of Steve Jobs stands as a captivating account of triumphing over challenges through groundbreaking ideas and foresight. Steve Jobs, one of the co-founders of Apple Inc., encountered major obstacles during his tenure, such as being removed from the company he played a pivotal role in establishing. In spite of facing this setback, Jobs showed remarkable resilience and ingenuity by establishing NeXT and subsequently acquiring Pixar. His return to Apple and the subsequent revival of the company through innovative products like the iPod, iPhone, and iPad highlight his capacity to adapt and reinvent himself in challenging circumstances. Jobs' story exemplifies the potential for transformative success through vision, creativity, and a willingness to take risks, despite enduring significant personal and professional setbacks.

An exemplary illustration of triumphing over challenges can

be observed in the life of Malala Yousafzai. Malala, a staunch advocate for girls' education in Pakistan, encountered significant resistance from the Taliban, who attempted to suppress her activism through acts of violence. In 2012, she endured an assassination attempt that resulted in severe injuries. In spite of this distressing incident, Malala persevered in her advocacy with heightened resolve. She later became the youngest-ever Nobel Prize laureate, utilizing her platform to advocate for education and equality on a global scale. The story of Malala serves as a powerful testament to the strength and determination displayed in the face of life-threatening challenges. Her steadfast dedication to her cause, despite the significant personal risk involved, serves as a source of inspiration for individuals advocating for justice and equality.

Another example that highlights how individuals can triumph over substantial physical challenges to live meaningful lives is the story of Nick Vujicic, a motivational speaker who was born without limbs. In spite of his congenital condition, Vujicic has traveled extensively, spreading a message of hope and resilience to millions of people worldwide. He inspires others to overcome their own challenges and pursue their dreams through his organization, Life Without Limbs. The story of Vujicic highlights the significance of maintaining a positive mindset and the profound influence that support networks can have in surmounting both physical and emotional obstacles. The life of this individual exemplifies the power of embracing one's unique circumstances and leveraging one's strengths to create a life of significance and influence.

Every one of these narratives, although distinct, revolves around similar themes of strength, perseverance, and the skill to transform challenges into chances. These narratives serve as a source of inspiration and offer valuable insights on how to overcome challenges. The significance of maintaining a positive outlook, seeking support from others, and staying committed to one's goals despite setbacks is emphasized. These principles can be applied in a wide range of contexts, including personal development, professional pursuits, and broader societal challenges.

Furthermore, the insights gleaned from these narratives can hold significant relevance in the context of our swiftly evolving society. Amidst the current global pandemic, economic uncertainty, and social upheaval, it is crucial to seek guidance from individuals and communities that have successfully overcome similar challenges. Their strategies can provide valuable insights for navigating these unprecedented times. Adaptability, perseverance, and innovation are essential qualities that individuals must possess in order to successfully navigate the complexities of modern life and accomplish their goals.

Stories of triumphing over challenges are compelling narratives that connect with the larger themes of personal accomplishment and effective strategies for achieving success. These stories demonstrate the relationship between personal resilience and the strategies used to overcome adversity, providing valuable insights for individuals looking to conquer their own challenges. By studying these narratives, individuals can develop the qualities needed to accomplish their goals and make significant contributions to their communities and the world.

Lessons Learned and Advice from ADHD Achievers

Living with ADHD (Attention-Deficit/Hyperactivity Disorder) poses distinct challenges that can affect multiple areas of life, including academic and professional accomplishments, personal relationships, and self-esteem. Many individuals with ADHD have successfully managed their symptoms and achieved significant success in their respective fields. Their stories provide valuable insights and practical advice for others who are navigating similar paths, demonstrating how the lessons they have learned can be applied to achieve personal and professional growth.

An important lesson that many individuals with ADHD have

learned is the value of accepting and embracing their unique neurodiversity. Instead of perceiving ADHD as a disabling condition, accomplished individuals often acknowledge it as a distinct cognitive style that can bring forth exceptional strengths, such as creativity, problem-solving abilities, and intense focus.

This change in viewpoint can be empowering, allowing individuals to utilize their skills and apply them efficiently. As an example, David Neeleman, the founder of JetBlue Airways, attributes his ADHD to his innovative thinking and knack for recognizing overlooked opportunities. Neeleman's acceptance of his ADHD allowed him to transform perceived weaknesses into strengths, leading to groundbreaking innovations in customer service and operational efficiency within the airline industry.

One important lesson we can learn from individuals who have achieved success despite having ADHD is the importance of implementing structure and organization. ADHD can pose challenges to maintaining focus and completing tasks. However, implementing effective organizational strategies can help mitigate these difficulties. Utilizing tools such as planners, reminders, and time-management apps can assist individuals in maintaining focus and meeting deadlines.

In addition, dividing tasks into smaller, more manageable steps can help alleviate feelings of being overwhelmed and enhance productivity. Structure and routine play a crucial role in Olympian Michael Phelps' training regimen, as he highlights their significance while managing ADHD. Through a commitment to a well-defined timetable and the establishment of achievable objectives, Phelps effectively directed his efforts, resulting in his remarkable achievements as one of the most accomplished athletes in history.

Support systems are essential for the success of individuals with ADHD. Having a robust support system, whether it be through family, friends, mentors, or professional networks, can offer valuable encouragement, guidance, and accountability. It is widely acknowledged by individuals who have achieved success despite having ADHD that seeking assistance when necessary and being willing to depend on others for support are crucial factors. Simone Biles, the esteemed Olympic gymnast, has openly shared her experience with ADHD and the invaluable support she received from her dedicated family and coaches.

This network not only assisted her in effectively managing her symptoms but also offered the necessary emotional and psychological support to thrive in her sport. The role of the support system in Biles' life highlights the importance of having understanding and supportive individuals around oneself.

In addition, having a strong sense of self-awareness and the ability to advocate for oneself are crucial elements in effectively managing life with ADHD. Having a clear understanding of one's strengths and weaknesses enables individuals to devise strategies that are customized to their unique requirements. Self-advocacy requires effectively expressing one's needs to others, whether in educational environments, professional settings, or personal relationships. Richard Branson, an entrepreneur with ADHD, frequently emphasizes the significance of self-awareness and advocates for appropriate accommodations and support. The individual's method of self-awareness has played a crucial role in their capacity to establish a varied and prosperous business empire.

ADHD achievers also highlight the significance of prioritizing both physical and mental well-being. Engaging in regular exercise, maintaining a balanced diet, and ensuring adequate sleep can have a significant impact on an individual's ability to effectively manage symptoms associated with ADHD. Research has demonstrated that engaging in physical activity can enhance concentration, decrease hyperactivity, and elevate mood. Emma Watson, an actress who has openly discussed her experiences with ADHD, implements mindfulness practices and physical exercise as part of her routine to effectively manage her symptoms. By placing a high value on their health, individuals can enhance their overall well-being and improve their ability to handle the challenges associated with ADHD. Another important lesson to consider is the need for flexibility and adaptability. Living with ADHD often necessitates adapting plans and strategies to accommodate the variability of attention spans and energy levels. Having the ability to adapt enables individuals to make necessary adjustments and explore alternative routes to accomplish their objectives. Daymond John, a renowned entrepreneur and philanthropist, credits a significant portion of his achievements to his remarkable capacity to adapt and persist in the face of challenges, including those presented by his ADHD. The narrative exemplifies how adaptability can result in creative resolutions and prospects that may not have been immediately evident.

Individuals with ADHD who have achieved success often emphasize the significance of pursuing their passions and leveraging their interests. Participating in activities that are in line with one's interests can boost motivation and concentration, thus facilitating the attainment of success. Ned Hallowell, an author and motivational speaker who has ADHD, emphasizes the importance of pursuing work and hobbies that bring joy and ignite passion. By aligning their pursuits with their interests, individuals can create a fulfilling and successful path that capitalizes on their unique strengths. Resilience is a vital lesson that can be learned from individuals who have achieved success despite living with ADHD. Dealing with and overcoming setbacks is a frequent occurrence, but having a resilient mindset enables individuals to persist through challenges. Resilience is typically developed by utilizing a combination of self-compassion, positive self-talk, and the assistance of others. Howie Mandel, an actor and comedian with ADHD, frequently emphasizes the significance of resilience in his career. Despite facing multiple obstacles, his resilience and unwavering commitment to his passions have been fundamental to his achievements.

The experiences of successful individuals with ADHD offer valuable insights and guidance for those facing their own challenges with ADHD. Embracing neurodiversity, implementing efficient organizational strategies, establishing robust support systems, and cultivating self-awareness and self-advocacy are all essential elements for achieving success. In order to overcome obstacles and achieve their goals, individuals with ADHD should prioritize their physical and mental health, be flexible and adaptable, pursue their passions, and cultivate resilience. These strategies are essential for success.

These narratives serve as both inspiration and practical guidance, demonstrating how individuals can transform the obstacles of ADHD into catalysts for personal development and achievement. By studying the experiences of individuals who have successfully managed their ADHD, people can gain valuable insights and practical strategies to improve their emotional and mental well-being.

CHAPTER 6

INTERACTIVE COMPONENTS

Tools and Worksheets for Self-Assessment

Developing self-awareness is crucial for personal development, particularly when navigating intricate emotional, mental, and behavioral terrains. Utilizing tools and worksheets for self-assessment is essential in this process. These resources offer individuals a methodical way to assess their thoughts, emotions, behaviors, and overall mental health, facilitating a structured process of self-reflection. Through the facilitation of self-awareness, these tools have the ability to assist individuals in recognizing their strengths and areas that require improvement. This guidance can ultimately lead them towards a life that is both healthier and more fulfilling.

There are different types of self-assessment tools available, such as questionnaires, checklists, rating scales, and reflective worksheets. Every type of therapy has a distinct purpose and is tailored to target specific aspects of an individual's mental and emotional well-being. For instance, widely utilized standardized questionnaires like the Beck Depression Inventory (BDI) or the Generalized Anxiety Disorder 7 (GAD-7) scale are employed for screening depression and anxiety, respectively. These tools offer a measurable way to assess symptoms, aiding individuals and healthcare providers in comprehending the extent of their conditions.

Reflective worksheets, however, promote a more profound level of self-examination. The worksheets typically contain prompts or questions that assist individuals in analyzing their emotions, actions, and thought processes. As an example, a cognitive-behavioral therapy (CBT) thought record worksheet may require individuals to record a particular event, their emotional reaction, the automatic thoughts that occurred, and alternative, more balanced thoughts they could contemplate. This exercise is designed to assist individuals in identifying and addressing negative thinking patterns, promoting cognitive restructuring and emotional regulation.

In addition, self-assessment tools can be highly advantageous for individuals managing chronic conditions or mental health disorders. These tools offer a valuable way to monitor symptoms and track progress over an extended period of time. For instance, individuals diagnosed with ADHD (Attention-Deficit/Hyperactivity Disorder) may utilize rating scales to track their levels of focus, impulsivity, and hyperactivity on a daily or weekly basis. Continuous monitoring can assist individuals and their healthcare providers in making more effective adjustments to treatment plans, thereby ensuring improved symptom management.

Interactive self-assessment tools utilize technology to improve user engagement and accuracy. Mobile applications and online platforms provide a variety of self-assessment features, including mood trackers and comprehensive mental health assessments. These digital tools frequently offer prompt feedback and tailored recommendations based on the user's responses, enhancing their accessibility and user-friendliness. Apps such as Moodfit or Youper provide daily mood tracking, cognitive-behavioral exercises, and meditation guides to assist users in proactively managing their mental health.

When considering self-assessment tools, it is crucial to maintain a discerning perspective. Although they can offer valuable insights, it is important to note that they should not be considered as replacements for professional diagnosis or treatment. It is important to have a discussion with a healthcare provider regarding the results of your self-assessment. This will help ensure that the interpretation is accurate and that appropriate action can be taken. In addition, it is important to consider the reliability and validity of the tools utilized. Utilizing tools that have been extensively validated in clinical settings can provide more precise and reliable outcomes.

Effectively utilizing self-assessment tools requires more than simply filling out worksheets or questionnaires. One must possess a strong dedication to integrity and introspection. It is essential for individuals to have the willingness to address uncomfortable truths regarding themselves and their behaviors. The process may present difficulties, but it is an essential component in achieving significant transformation. For example, utilizing a stress diary to record daily stressors and coping mechanisms can reveal patterns and triggers that may not have been consciously recognized. Identifying these patterns is the initial stage in cultivating more effective coping mechanisms and diminishing stress levels.

In addition, incorporating self-assessment into a more comprehensive self-care regimen can improve its efficacy. One way to enhance self-awareness and improve emotional regulation is by combining self-assessment with mindfulness practices. Mindfulness promotes the practice of observing thoughts and feelings without passing judgment, allowing individuals to process and gain a deeper understanding of their self-assessment results. Through the integration of these methods, individuals have the opportunity to develop a more empathetic and comprehensive approach to their mental well-being.

Self-assessment tools are commonly used by educators and therapists to enhance the empowerment of their clients and students. These tools are designed to enhance communication and promote effective collaboration in goal-setting. Learning style inventories are commonly used in educational settings to assist students in identifying their preferred methods of learning. This information allows teachers to customize their instruction to better meet the needs of each student. In the same way, therapists utilize self-assessment worksheets to assist clients in clearly expressing their objectives and monitoring their advancement in therapy. This approach encourages individuals to take ownership of their personal development journey by fostering collaboration.

In addition, self-assessment tools have the potential to foster a growth mindset. Through consistent self-evaluation and the establishment of small, achievable goals, individuals can cultivate a more optimistic and proactive mindset towards their personal development. For example, a strengths and weaknesses analysis worksheet can assist individuals in identifying their areas of expertise and areas that may require additional effort. Adopting a balanced perspective fosters a culture of continuous learning and resilience, as individuals understand that their abilities can be enhanced through dedication and effort.

To successfully incorporate self-assessment into your daily routine, it is important to allocate dedicated time for consistent reflection and review. Maintaining consistency is crucial for obtaining valuable insights from self-assessment tools. Creating a regular schedule, such as a weekly self-evaluation, can help maintain a focus on self-assessment. During these check-ins, participants have the opportunity to review their worksheets, engage in self-reflection regarding their progress, and establish new goals for the upcoming week. Implementing this practice not only ensures individual accountability but also fosters a clear sense of direction and purpose.

Ultimately, self-assessment has the potential to cultivate a sense of self-compassion. As individuals develop greater self-awareness, they can cultivate a mindset of self-acceptance and recognize their personal growth. Self-assessment involves acknowledging areas for improvement and acknowledging progress made, rather than focusing on faults or shortcomings. By adopting a compassionate approach, individuals can effectively reduce self-criticism and cultivate a healthier and more positive self-image.

Self-assessment tools and worksheets are highly valuable resources that can greatly aid individuals in their pursuit of self-awareness and personal growth. They offer a systematic method for assessing one's mental and emotional condition, identifying recurring patterns and triggers, and monitoring progress over time.

When utilized properly and with the guidance of experts, these tools can enable individuals to make well-informed decisions regarding their mental health and overall well-being.Through the incorporation of self-assessment into a comprehensive self-care regimen and the dedication to sincere self-reflection, individuals can cultivate a more empathetic and proactive mindset towards their personal growth.

Activities and Exercises with Guidance

Interactive components are essential for increasing engagement and facilitating learning in a variety of fields, such as education, training, therapy, and self-improvement. Activities and exercises with guidance are highly effective tools for promoting active participation, fostering skill development, and deepening understanding among these components.

Our program offers a variety of activities and exercises that provide clear guidance and promote interactive experiences. These opportunities are specifically designed to facilitate hands-on learning and help participants acquire new skills. These activities are typically organized and accompanied by clear instructions, prompts, or feedback to effectively guide participants through the process. Whether conducted in a classroom, workshop, therapy session, or self-guided study, these activities provide a dynamic and immersive approach to engaging with content and concepts.

Activities and exercises with guidance are frequently employed in educational settings to reinforce lessons, foster critical thinking, and evaluate comprehension. As an illustration, a science teacher could arrange a lab experiment to showcase a concept that has been covered in class. The teacher would offer students precise instructions and assistance throughout the entire process. In language learning, interactive exercises like role-plays, games, and simulations provide students with a supportive environment to practice speaking, listening, and writing.

Professional training and development utilize activities and exercises with guidance to cultivate essential skills and competencies. For example, a leadership workshop typically incorporates various activities such as team-building exercises, case studies, and role-playing scenarios. These activities aim to enhance participants' communication, problem-solving, and decision-making abilities. Feedback and debriefing sessions play a crucial role in these activities, enabling participants to analyze their performance and pinpoint areas that need improvement.

Activities and exercises are employed in therapeutic settings to facilitate personal growth, emotional healing, and behavior change with the guidance of professionals. As an illustration, a therapist specializing in anxiety treatment may employ guided relaxation techniques, breathing exercises, and exposure therapy to assist clients in effectively managing their symptoms. These activities offer a structured and supportive approach that enables clients to practice coping strategies in a safe and controlled environment.

In addition, engaging in activities and exercises with proper guidance can be highly beneficial for enhancing one's skills and fostering personal growth. Interactive components are often integrated into self-help books, online courses, and coaching programs to improve learning and engagement. For example, a self-help book on stress management may provide journaling prompts, reflection exercises, and goal-setting activities to assist readers in applying the discussed concepts to their personal lives.

Activities and exercises with guidance are highly effective in promoting active learning and participation. Active engagement with the material enhances participants' ability to retain information, develop skills, and apply their learning in real-world contexts. In addition, the guidance offered during these activities assists in structuring learning, guaranteeing that participants remain focused and receive assistance when necessary.

Also, providing activities and exercises with clear guidance can accommodate a wide range of learning styles and preferences. Interactive diagrams, charts, and videos can be helpful for visual learners, while hands-on activities and role-playing exercises may be more suitable for kinesthetic learners. Through the provision of a diverse range of interactive experiences, individuals in the fields of education, training, therapy, and content creation can effectively cater to the requirements of various learners and optimize levels of engagement.

Activities and exercises that provide guidance have the potential to not only promote learning and skill development but also foster collaboration, communication, and social interaction. Collaborative activities, discussions, and problem-solving exercises foster a sense of teamwork, facilitate the exchange of ideas, and promote mutual learning among participants. This approach fosters a collaborative environment that not only improves the learning experience but also develops crucial interpersonal skills necessary for success in personal and professional settings.

In addition, activities and exercises can be customized to target specific learning objectives, therapeutic goals, or skill-building needs while providing clear guidance. For instance, a workshop on conflict resolution could incorporate role-playing exercises and guided discussions that center around effective communication and negotiation strategies. In therapy sessions for individuals with social anxiety, exposure exercises and guided visualization techniques are often used to assist clients in conquering their fears.

Activities and exercises, when accompanied by guidance, are highly valuable interactive components. They have the ability to enhance engagement, promote learning, and facilitate skill development in various contexts. Interactive experiences can be utilized in various fields such as education, training, therapy, or self-improvement. They provide a dynamic and immersive approach to engaging with content and concepts. Through the provision of structure, support, and feedback, activities and exercises with guidance enable participants to actively engage in their own learning and personal growth journey.

QR Codes for Video and Extra Resource Information

In the modern era of technology, interactive elements are essential for increasing user engagement and providing easy access to supplementary resources and information. QR codes have become a versatile tool for connecting users to multimedia content, supplementary materials, and extended learning resources, among other components. By integrating QR codes into different contexts, such as educational materials, marketing campaigns, and product packaging, organizations and content creators can provide users with a smooth and interactive experience that enhances their understanding and engagement.

QR codes, also known as Quick Response codes, are a type of two-dimensional barcode that can be easily scanned using a smartphone or tablet with a camera and a QR code reader application. The codes are composed of black modules organized in a square grid on a white background. They are used to encode various types of information, including text, URLs, and other data. QR codes have the ability to initiate a range of actions when scanned, including opening websites, displaying text or images, playing videos, or downloading files.

QR codes have a significant role in granting access to video content and additional resources. As an illustration, educational materials like textbooks, worksheets, and study guides can incorporate QR codes that direct users to instructional videos, interactive tutorials, and multimedia presentations. Through the utilization of QR codes, students are provided with the opportunity to access supplementary explanations, demonstrations, and examples that effectively enhance their learning experience and solidify fundamental concepts.

In marketing and advertising, QR codes are frequently utilized to offer consumers access to product demonstrations, testimonials, and promotional videos. For example, product packaging, brochures, and posters often include QR codes that direct users to product demonstration videos, customer reviews, or exclusive offers. By scanning these QR codes, individuals can enhance their understanding of the product or service and make well-informed purchasing decisions.

In addition, QR codes are commonly used in museums, galleries, and cultural institutions to offer visitors access to supplementary information, audio guides, and interactive exhibits. QR codes can be utilized to provide comprehensive information about artworks, artifacts, and exhibits. These codes can be scanned to access detailed descriptions, historical context, and multimedia content. Visitors can use their smartphones or tablets to scan these QR codes and explore supplementary materials that enhance their understanding and appreciation of the exhibits.

QR codes are being used more and more in the publishing industry to enhance print materials like books, magazines, and newspapers. They provide readers with convenient access to digital content, author interviews, and related articles. For instance, a magazine article discussing a new technology may incorporate a QR code that directs readers to a video demonstration or an interview with the inventor. Readers can gain a deeper understanding of the topic and access additional insights and perspectives by scanning the QR code.

QR codes are also utilized in event management and

conference settings to offer attendees access to event agendas, speaker bios, presentation slides, and networking opportunities. Event programs, badges, and signage can include QR codes that direct attendees to event-specific apps, websites, or social media platforms. This allows them to access pertinent information and engage with fellow participants.

QR codes provide a convenient and effective method for enhancing user engagement and granting access to supplementary resources and information. QR codes have proven to be highly effective in various industries, including education, marketing, cultural institutions, publishing, and event management. They provide users with a seamless way to access multimedia content, supplementary materials, and extended resources, enhancing their experience and fostering a deeper understanding. Through the utilization of QR codes as interactive elements, organizations and content creators have the ability to develop immersive and captivating experiences that deeply resonate with users and significantly enhance their overall satisfaction.

CHAPTER 7

The Way to a Successful ADHD Life in Conclusion

Formulating a Customized Action Plan

Creating a tailored action plan is crucial to effectively managing attention deficit hyperactivity disorder (ADHD). This personalized roadmap is designed to provide clear guidance for individuals with ADHD, taking into account their specific strengths, challenges, and goals. It aims to assist them in effectively navigating the complexities of daily life. An effective action plan includes a variety of strategies, interventions, and resources aimed at improving functioning, promoting growth, and boosting overall well-being. Individuals with ADHD can develop a sense of empowerment, resilience, and success by focusing on important aspects such as organization, time management, emotional regulation, and self-care.

An essential aspect of developing a tailored action plan involves engaging in self-assessment and reflection. It is important to develop a thorough understanding of an individual's strengths, weaknesses, preferences, and needs in different areas of life that are impacted by ADHD. By engaging in self-reflection exercises, journaling, and having discussions with trusted individuals like family members, friends, or mental health professionals, individuals can effectively identify patterns, triggers, and areas for improvement. By recognizing the obstacles and identifying areas for improvement, individuals can establish a solid groundwork for creating specific strategies and interventions that are customized to their individual circumstances.

After identifying the key areas of focus, the next step is to establish specific and attainable goals for formulating a customized action plan. The goals should be practical, quantifiable, and in line with the individual's values, priorities, and aspirations. Breaking down goals into smaller, manageable steps can make them more attainable and sustainable, whether the aim is to improve time management skills, enhance academic performance, or strengthen relationships. Incorporating elements of motivation, accountability, and reward can assist individuals in maintaining their commitment to their goals and monitoring their progress over time.

When developing strategies and interventions to support goal attainment, it is crucial to rely on evidence-based practices and interventions that have demonstrated effectiveness in managing ADHD symptoms. Some possible interventions may include cognitive-behavioral therapy (CBT), executive function coaching, or mindfulness-based techniques. In addition, making lifestyle adjustments, such as engaging in regular physical activity, getting enough sleep, and maintaining a balanced diet, can significantly contribute to enhancing overall well-being and optimizing brain function. In addition, individuals can enhance their productivity, organization, and time management by utilizing technology and assistive tools. One way to effectively manage your time is by utilizing various tools, such as smartphone apps, digital calendars, or task management tools. These tools can help you set reminders, create schedules, and track your progress on goals and tasks. In challenging environments, individuals can utilize tools like noise-canceling headphones, fidget toys, or sensory accommodations to effectively manage sensory sensitivities and maintain focus.

Incorporating self-care practices that promote mental, emotional, and physical well-being is a crucial component of a personalized action plan. Engaging in activities that promote relaxation, stress reduction, and emotional regulation can be beneficial. Examples include meditation, deep breathing exercises, or engaging in hobbies that bring joy and fulfillment. In addition, implementing regular routines and rituals, nurturing social connections, and seeking guidance from peers and professionals can assist individuals in developing resilience, managing difficulties, and cultivating a feeling of belonging and community.

It is crucial for individuals to consistently monitor their

progress, evaluate the effectiveness of their customized action plans, and make any necessary adjustments. It is important to monitor adherence to strategies, evaluate any changes in symptoms or functioning, and gather feedback from reliable sources. Through maintaining a flexible and open-minded mindset, individuals can continuously refine their approach, leveraging successes, learning from setbacks, and consistently striving for growth and improvement.

Developing a tailored action plan is a crucial step in the path to achieving success and fulfillment for individuals with ADHD. Through the process of self-assessment, the establishment of achievable goals, and the utilization of evidence-based strategies and interventions, individuals have the ability to leverage their strengths, address obstacles, and enhance their overall quality of life.

By engaging in continuous self-reflection, making necessary adjustments, and prioritizing personal well-being, individuals can effectively navigate the challenges associated with ADHD. This approach fosters resilience, boosts confidence, and cultivates a strong sense of purpose. By following a meticulously designed action plan, individuals can begin their journey towards a prosperous and satisfying life. This will enable them to conquer challenges and fully realize their capabilities.

Maintaining Motivation and Rejoicing in Achievements

It is crucial to emphasize the importance of staying motivated and celebrating accomplishments when managing the challenges of living with attention deficit hyperactivity disorder (ADHD). Individuals with ADHD frequently experience challenges in maintaining motivation and acknowledging their achievements, especially in the presence of obstacles and setbacks. Through the implementation of effective strategies, the cultivation of a growth mindset, and the fostering of a supportive environment, individuals can successfully overcome obstacles, maintain motivation, and ultimately experience the satisfaction of achieving their goals.

An important strategy for maintaining motivation is to establish goals that are both realistic and attainable. Breaking down larger objectives into smaller, manageable tasks allows individuals to create a roadmap for success and effectively track their progress. Establishing goals that are specific, measurable, attainable, relevant, and time-bound (SMART) offers clarity and guidance, enabling individuals to maintain focus and motivation. Incorporating elements of intrinsic motivation, such as pursuing activities that align with personal interests and values, can significantly enhance engagement and enthusiasm.

In addition, individuals can enhance their motivation by utilizing external rewards and incentives. Recognizing accomplishments, whether they are small victories or significant milestones, can serve as a powerful motivator and encourage individuals to maintain their positive behaviors. In addition, it can be beneficial to share your achievements with trusted individuals, such as friends, family members, or mentors. This can offer you both encouragement and validation, which can boost your motivation and create a stronger sense of connection.

To effectively maintain motivation, it is essential to address various factors, such as managing distractions, overcoming procrastination, and cultivating resilience in the face of adversity. These elements, in addition to setting goals and celebrating achievements, play a crucial role in sustaining motivation. One approach to consider is the implementation of strategies like breaking tasks into smaller steps, creating structured routines, and minimizing environmental distractions. In addition, incorporating mindfulness, meditation, or other relaxation techniques into one's routine can assist individuals in maintaining focus and composure, particularly in demanding circumstances.

In addition, it is essential to develop a growth mindset in order to maintain motivation and view challenges as chances for personal development and learning. Instead of perceiving setbacks as failures, individuals have the ability to reframe them as valuable learning experiences and opportunities to enhance their strategies and skills. By adopting a constructive mindset and having confidence in their capacity to surmount challenges, individuals can sustain their motivation and persist in the pursuit of their objectives.

Creating an environment that supports growth, acknowledges progress, and offers encouragement is crucial for maintaining motivation. Having a strong support system consisting of friends, family members, or mentors can offer emotional support, accountability, and inspiration. In addition, it can be beneficial to connect with communities or support groups comprised of individuals who have ADHD. Doing so can foster a sense of belonging and empathy, which can help alleviate feelings of isolation and boost motivation.

To summarize, it is crucial to maintain motivation and celebrate accomplishments in order to lead a successful life with ADHD. By establishing attainable objectives, acknowledging successes, minimizing interruptions, developing mental fortitude, and creating a nurturing atmosphere, individuals can maintain their drive and derive satisfaction from their accomplishments. Individuals with ADHD can successfully navigate life's challenges, overcome obstacles, and thrive in pursuit of their goals and aspirations through dedication, perseverance, and a positive mindset.